Exploring tough questions facing youth today

CLUELESS AND CALLED

Discipleship and the Gospel of Mark

The Pastoral Center

ISBN 978-1-949628-07-4
Printed in the United States of America.
10 9 8 7 6 5 4 3 2 1   22 21 20 19

Published by The Pastoral Center, http://pastoral.center.

Developed in partnership with MennoMedia and Brethren Press. Series editors: Fumiaki Tosu, Ann Naffziger, and Paul Canavese. *Clueless and Called:* Writer, Robbie Miller. Project editor, Lani Wright. Staff editors, Susan E. Janzen, Julie Garber, and James Deaton. Updated design, Paul Stocksdale.

All rights reserved. Purchase of this book includes a license to reproduce this resource for use in a single parish, school, or other similar organization. You are allowed to share and make unlimited copies only for use within the organization that licensed it. If you serve more than one organization, each should purchase its own license. You may not post this document to any web site without explicit permission to do so. Outside of these conditions, no part of this book may be reproduced in any form or by any means, electronic or mechanical, including photocopying, recording, taping, or via any retrieval system, without the written permission of The Pastoral Center, 1212 Versailles Ave., Alameda, CA 94501. Thank you for cooperating with our honor system regarding our licenses.

For questions or to order additional copies or licenses, please call 1-844-727-8672 or visit http://pastoral.center.

Portions of this work © 2019 by The Pastoral Center / PastoralCenter.com. Adapted and published with permission from Generation Why Bible Studies. © 1996, 2014 Brethren Press, Elgin, IL 60120 and MennoMedia, Harrisonburg, VA 22803, U.S.A. All rights reserved.

Unless otherwise noted, the Scripture passages contained herein are from the *New Revised Standard Version of the Bible*, copyright © 1989 by the National Council of the Churches of Christ in the United States of America. Used by permission. All rights reserved.

Bible-based Explorations of Issues Facing Youth

» OVERVIEW

When conversing online, the acronym IRL stands for "in real life." The virtual world of social media, text chats, blogs, and more have the power to remove us from the real world. What we experience online can skew our perspective on what it means to be human. It can numb us, incite us, distract us, depress us, confuse us, and make us rude or impatient. Strangely, this supposedly "social" and "connected" technology can profoundly disconnect us from others.

Religious faith can also place us in a bubble, especially when it distances us from others. When we keep the prophetic message at a safe distance, obscured in theological language and abstractions, we are missing the whole point. And when we see our parish as an insider club that serves itself, we can forget the radically inclusive message entrusted to us: God's love is for *everyone*, and God expects us to transform the *whole world* through that love.

Through the incarnation, God showed up in the real world to show us that our faith is not just about talking the talk, but also walking the walk. It can be risky. It can be confusing. It can hurt. But living out our faith can also bring us great purpose, peace, and joy.

This series connects the Bible with the tough questions that youth (and adults) encounter in their neighborhood, in school, among friends, and even online. This process will help you as a leader break open these issues in a fun and meaningful way, sparking conversation and the kind of life change Jesus invites us to embrace.

» THE ROLE OF PARENTS

As children enter middle school and high school, they become more independent, self-reliant, and, well, self-centered. This can bring parents to make assumptions that this is the time to step back, giving their child more space to form their identity. While there is truth to that at some level (adolescents definitely shouldn't be smothered), this is a stage of life when parents should in fact *lean in*. The apparent confidence and bluster youth show on the outside can mask the insecurity and confusion on the inside. Youth need their parents to be involved more than ever.

» WHOLE FAMILY FORMATION

Parents are the primary teachers of their own children, and parishes are waking up to the fact that faith formation programs need to bring parents into the process if they hope to see faith passed on to the next generation. Recent studies give us more and more evidence that the role of parents is the most important factor in determining whether a child will embrace faith as they move toward adulthood. Research from the Center for the Applied Research on the Apostolate shows that parents who talk about their faith and show through their actions that their faith is important to them are more likely to have children who remain Catholic.

More about Whole Family Formation »»»

To learn more about how your parish can take a comprehensive whole family approach to faith formation, visit **GrowingUpCatholic.com**.

While whole family events with elementary-aged children are on the rise, the role of parents can be an afterthought in youth ministry. We have designed the sessions in this series to work with or without parents present, and we encourage you to offer them as parent-child events.

If you choose to involve parents, it is important to consider before each session how to best do so. Many of the activities in this series are high-energy, creative, or silly. Some parents may need some encouragement to get out of their heads and have fun with the group. A few activities involving physical contact would be inappropriate for parents and youth to participate together, and we have noted them as such.

There are a number of ways to approach discussions with parent participation. Unless you have a small group, you will likely want to break into smaller groups for conversation. Some youth may be self-conscious and unable to be completely honest and open in a group situation with a parent present. For this reason, you may choose in some cases to assign parents to different groups from their own children, or to have separate parent and child groups altogether. Be sure to cover expectations around confidentiality. It is inappropriate for a parent (or youth) to share with another parent what their child said in a small group.

Note that even if parents and their children do not share all conversations together in the session, they will still have a valuable shared experience and can have extended conversations about it later.

»» THANK YOU

The role you play in gathering, animating, praying with, and forming youth is a valuable one. Thank you for all you do to serve the church and its families!

Bible-based Explorations of Issues Facing Youth

CLUELESS AND CALLED
Discipleship and the Gospel of Mark

>> INTRODUCTION

In the New Testament, "disciples" are most often the followers of Jesus, including the twelve closest to him plus a wide range of others.

Simple enough. But what does it take to be one? According to the Gospel of Mark, it takes more *and less* than we might think. *Less*, because as Jesus' twelve disciples demonstrate so well, we don't need great or perfect faith. *More*, because the way of Jesus is the way of the disciple, and those who truly follow this suffering Messiah will always pay a high price.

The Gospel of Mark was probably written in Rome after the death of Peter and during Nero's persecution of Christians (beginning 64 C.E., or "Common Era"). Most scholars agree that Mark was the earliest Gospel and a primary source for both Matthew and Luke. Even though it was anonymous, ancient tradition identifies the author as John Mark, Peter's companion in Rome, who wrote it as a summary of Peter's preaching. The Gospel's purpose is to show Jesus Christ as the Son of God who proclaims and embodies the realm of God. Moreover, Mark's vision of this Christ is meant to inspire readers to follow in Jesus' sacrificial way.

Despite a fairly clear purpose, however, Mark unashamedly depicts those closest to Jesus, the disciples, as being distinctly *unclear* about Jesus' purpose. When Jesus laid his hands on the blind man at Bethsaida and asked if he could see anything, the man responded, "I can see people, but they look like trees, walking" (8:24). Only after Jesus touched him a second time was his sight restored so that "he saw everything clearly" (8:25). Like the man's physical blindness, the disciples' spiritual blindness throughout the Gospel kept them from seeing clearly the truth about Jesus, though he "touched" them time and time again. They had enormous trouble "clueing in."

Jesus anguished over their inability to see. "Do you not yet understand?" (8:21). Yet he loved and forgave his disciples, constantly calling them to "follow me" (1:17). That's good news for modern-day disciples who see no more clearly than the first twelve, but want to follow where Jesus leads.

Bombarded from all sides by society's priorities of conformity, popularity, prosperity, self-gratification, and success, today's youth are understandably confused about which messages to believe, what values to choose, and which of many self-proclaimed "saviors" to follow. The

Preparation Alert >>>>

Sessions 1, 2, and 5 ask for you to contact people for specific tasks ahead of time. Begin making those contacts now.

If you plan to use the extender session, arrange to view the video. (See order information in Extender Session.)

››› EXTENDER SESSION

Most units include one extender session, with suggestions for special activities related to the issue of the unit. Extender sessions help accommodate the diversity of parish schedules. Since each unit is undated, participants may study units in their entirety and still participate in special events of the parish that get scheduled simultaneously with youth group time. Extender sessions can be used anytime, but the one for this unit best follows **Session 4**. Calculate now whether or not you will be using the extender session.

church has often failed to *touch* our youth once, much less twice, and has left them to stumble about blindly in the virtual reality of popular culture.

According to Mark, Jesus came as the world's true Messiah and called uncertain disciples to get in the boat and set out to sea; to drop their nets and follow him; to deny themselves and experience "the good life" of God's realm; to travel light as they continued his work in the world; and to be disciples in a way that required genuine repentance and commitment, *not moral perfection*. This is the call our participants need to hear. This is the call the sessions of this unit are designed to help you convey.

Unlike the blind man whom Jesus touched twice, our sight may still be faulty, our minds relatively clueless. But even if we never see everything as clearly as the man with restored sight, we can follow where Jesus leads. Following Jesus is what discipleship, and this unit, are all about.

THE TEACHING PLAN: The parts of the session guide

- ›› **Faith story.** The session is rooted in this Bible passage.
- ›› **Faith focus.** This is the story of the passage in a nutshell.
- ›› **Session goal.** The entire session is built around this goal. What changes—in knowledge, attitude, and/or action—do you desire in your group?
- ›› **Materials needed and advance preparation.** This is what you will need if the session is to go smoothly. You'll feel more at ease if you've taken care of these details before you meet your group.

›› FROM LIFE TO BIBLE TO LIFE

The teaching plan we use is called *life-centered*. However, when we write each session, we always begin with scripture. We ask, what does this particular passage say, especially to youth? Each session moves from life to Bible to life. So the Bible is really at the center of this way of teaching.

In every session we try to hit upon a tough question that participants might ask. Find out what questions on this issue are important for your group. Feel free to bring your own input and invite your group members to add their own experiences.

» TEACHING THE SESSION

The five step-by-step movements will carry you from *life to the Bible and back to life*. Each session takes about 45 to 50 minutes. If there is a handout sheet for the session, take note of any complementary activities and stories.

1. **Focus.** Intended to create a friendly climate within the group and to *draw attention* to the issue.

2. **Connect.** Invites participants to *express* their own life experience about the issue, through talking, drawing, role playing, and other activities. Also use memory, reason, or imagination to get the group thinking about *why* they view the issue the way they do.

3. **Explore the Bible.** What does the Bible *say* about the issue? With a minimum of lecturing, dig into the faith story and search for answers to questions raised in the first two movements. The Insights from Scripture section will help clarify the faith story. Help participants discover how the faith community understands the Bible passage.

4. **Apply the faith story.** What does the Bible passage *mean* for contemporary life? This is the "aha!" moment when learners realize the faith story has wisdom for *their* lives.

5. **Respond.** Why does the Bible passage *matter*? What will the group do about the issue in light of what they have learned from their own experiences set alongside the faith story? At this point, the faith story becomes *lived* rather than a mere intellectual exercise.

» LOOK AHEAD

Here are reminders for what you need to do for the next session or two.

» INSIGHTS FROM SCRIPTURE

Here is a resource for Explore the Bible. Don't try to use all the material given. Take what you need to lead the session and answer questions your group may have. Let the Insights section inspire you to think and study more about the Bible passage for the session.

» HANDOUT SHEETS

Occasionally, there will be a handout sheet to complement your session. If you choose to use this, make enough copies for the group in advance of the session. These sheets may include questions, stories, agree/disagree exercises, charts, pictures, and other materials to stimulate thinking and discussion.

Generally, no participant preparation is required unless the session plan calls for you to contact selected group members for specific tasks.

» MAIN SOURCES

Barclay, William. *The Gospel of Mark*.
Williamson, Lamar, Jr. *Interpretation: Mark*.

>>> SESSION 1

SEA-ING IS NOT ALWAYS BELIEVING >>>

>> KEY VERSE

And they were filled with great awe and said to one another, "Who then is this, that even the wind and the sea obey him?" (Mark 4:41)

>> FAITH STORY

Mark 4:35-41

>> FAITH FOCUS

After a long day teaching the crowds, Jesus and his disciples took a boat toward the other side of the Sea of Galilee. When a great storm blew in and threatened to sink the boat, the disciples frantically woke a snoozing Jesus and questioned his compassion for them. After Jesus calmed the wind and the sea with a word, the disciples were left awestruck and nervously wondering who this wonder-worker really was.

>> SESSION GOAL

Challenge participants to look for ways and reasons to trust Jesus more, on whatever sea and in whatever weather they are sailing.

>> Materials needed and advance preparation

- Contact three participants and assign parts for the game show "Ambiguity" (*Option A* in Focus).
- Copies of the handout sheets for Session 1
- Chalkboard/chalk or newsprint/marker
- Bibles
- Pencils/pens
- Blank note cards or index cards (Respond)

TEACHING PLAN

1. FOCUS 7 minutes

>> **Option A:** Contact three participants in advance and assign the parts of **Announcer**, **Contestant 1**, and **Contestant 2**; you serve as **Host**. You will need copies of the script "Welcome to … Ambiguity!" (on the first handout sheet) for them.

After the short skit, go on to **Option A** under Connect.

>> **Option B:** Using the handout sheet section titled "Disciple Ingredients," begin by having one of your more animated youth read the introduction. Or, simply start by saying something like:

*The media has always portrayed our cultural heroes, from Mother Teresa to LeBron James, as almost superhuman beings with few, if any, flaws. What qualities and characteristics do you think are really **necessary** to be a disciple, a follower of Jesus? List them on the chalkboard or newsprint under the heading, DISCIPLE INGREDIENTS.*

Go on to **Option B** under Connect.

2. CONNECT 7-9 minutes

>> **Option A:** Now ask:

- *What's "wrong" with this game show?*
- *When was the last time **you** were rewarded or affirmed for giving the wrong answer, expressing confusion, or admitting some doubt?*
- *What does this suggest about how society tends to regard doubt and confusion?*
- *What do **you** say about the pros and cons of doubt and confusion?*

>> **Option B:** Ask everyone to think about a time when they felt "put down" for giving a wrong answer, asking a question, expressing confusion, or admitting some doubt. Now write the following statement on the chalkboard or newsprint and ask each person to complete it verbally with one word: *When I was put down for not knowing it "all," I felt....* (**Note:** With this and all exercises, encourage participation, but allow people to pass if they wish.) List their words under the statement. When everyone has had a chance to share, ask:

- *Why did you feel the way you did?*
- *How did the experience make you feel about offering answers, asking questions, expressing confusion, or admitting doubts **again**?*
- *What do these feelings suggest about how society tends to regard doubt and confusion?*
- *What do **you** say about the pros and cons of doubt and confusion?*

3. EXPLORE THE BIBLE 13-15 minutes

Shift to this activity by saying: *If you're sometimes confused and full of doubts, you'll relate to some guys in the Bible who seemed mostly clueless about who Jesus was, even though they saw him preach, teach, and even perform miracles almost every day. And these guys were the disciples!*

Have everyone turn to Mark 4:35-41 and ask for a volunteer to read as they follow along. Then go directly to the discussion questions below, or enhance the Bible reading by passing out copies of "Not Your Everyday Boat Ride" (on the second handout sheet). Assign parts, with you being the narrator to keep the action moving. Ask two or more of your more uninhibited participants to be the "Crowd." After the reading, ask:

- *For the disciples, was getting into the boat with Jesus like getting into a car with a stranger? Were they stupid to do it? Why or why not?*
- *How did the reading make you feel about the crowd? About the disciples? About Jesus?*
- *How did the reading make you feel about your own questions, confusion, and doubts about Jesus?*
- *How did the reading make you feel about following Jesus **before** all of your questions about him are answered?*
- *Does following Jesus require a "watertight faith" or a simple, personal decision to "get in the boat" with him? Why or why not?*

CONFUSION REIGNS...

In your experience, how does the church tend to regard doubt and confusion? Are doubt and confusion weaknesses to overcome, or necessary parts of the learning process? What do you say about the pros and cons of doubt and confusion?

4. APPLY 7 minutes

Invite everyone to close their eyes, relax, and sit quietly as you slowly read the following guide to help them imagine the windstorm scene. Pause at each break:

*Imagine **you** are in a boat, sailing across a calm, still lake, with Jesus sleeping on a pillow in the stern.*

A great windstorm suddenly arises and waves beat into the boat so fiercely that it's swamped and in danger of sinking.

Now, imagine that the "windstorm" is something in your life that is threatening to overwhelm you, to harm you, to "sink your boat."

Try to identify what the "windstorm" is in your life. These also might be times when you felt Jesus was asleep on you. (Pause for a few moments.)

Feeling the end is near, you rush over to Jesus, shake him hard, and desperately yell, "Wake up, Jesus! Don't you care about me?"

Jesus wakes up, sees the fear in your eyes, then rebukes the wind and says to the sea, "Peace! Be still!"

Suddenly, you notice that your "windstorm," the situation that was creating so much pain, anxiety, or fear for you, is beginning to ease up and settle down into a peaceful calm once again.

Amazed, you turn to Jesus and see the fire in his eyes as he says, "Why are you afraid? Have you still no faith after all I have done for you?"

Only then do you realize that these are not words of impatient anger, but words of impatient love, spoken by One who yearns to be with you ...to be near you ...to be real to you.

In gratitude, you reach out to touch him, to thank him, to believe in him...and he's gone.

Confused, you look but see only your empty boat and calm waters all around.

*Filled with wonder, you say to yourself, "Who **was** this?"*

*And deep within, you know there's something here so real, so true, and so good that all the questions, confusion, and doubt in the world will **never** take it away.*

You don't understand him; at times you still doubt; but this much you know: He calls you to follow and find out more.

5. RESPOND 10 minutes

Distribute blank note cards or index cards. Invite everyone to write a simple, honest prayer beginning with the words, "Dear Jesus, in the windstorms of my life when I'm confused and afraid...." When everyone is done, suggest that they put this card in or near a place where they would see it often (on bedroom door, inside school locker, etc.).

(**Option:** Suggest the above "prayer card" be inserted as a prompt in cell phones, for participants who prefer to use reminders this way.)

Explain that the session will conclude with a brief, directed prayer in which you will offer several phrases and pause as they pray. Use or adapt the prayer on the second handout sheet (also in sidebar on this page).

Dear Jesus,
  when the wind is great,
  when the sea is high,
  when our boats are swamped,
  when our cries for help seem to go unheard,
  help us believe...
Dear Jesus,
  when our fear is great,
  when our confusion is high,
  when our doubts are pouring in,
  when our questions go unanswered, help us follow...
Dear Jesus,
  when the winds have died,
  when the sea has stilled,
  when our storm is over,
  help us see your love for us at work...
Dear Jesus,
  go with each one here into the time ahead,
  *resting in the stern of **our** boats,*
  ready to calm our windstorms whenever we call. AMEN.

>>> LOOK AHEAD

For next session, contact someone (not in your youth group) to knock on the meeting room door or call on the phone (*Option A* in Focus).

INSIGHTS FROM SCRIPTURE

A natural human reaction to distress or danger is to cry out to God. We may doubt there is a God. We may wonder if God cares or even knows about our problems. This passage is about that natural human reaction and God's response to it.

>> IN CONTROL

The disciples, to whom Jesus had just "explained everything in private" (4:34), apparently weren't getting the message. In a violent windstorm, as their boat was being swamped, they desperately tried to "jump start" a response from their sleeping teacher. In stark contrast to their sheer panic, Jesus was asleep, indicating here, as elsewhere in the Bible, a posture of complete trust in God.

"Peace! Be still!" Jesus used the same command to call out an unclean spirit from the demoniac (1:25) that he used to calm the storm (4:39). This suggests, says William Barclay, the ancient belief that demons were at work in the storm. The dramatic effect of Jesus' simple command on the storm was Mark's way of declaring his divine authority and control over demonic forces.

>> UNCOMFORTABLE GOOD NEWS

Though we might prefer to ignore Jesus' stern reproach (4:40), we must acknowledge his frustration, even impatience, with his disciples' lack of faith and understanding after so much time together. They were still clueless. What teacher wouldn't shake his head in despair? But more important is the fact that Jesus was *in the boat* with his disciples and *acted to save them* in spite of their thick-headed, fearful, and faith-less behavior. We might expect that Jesus' stilling of the raging storm might inspire his disciples to better faith—that they might nervously slap each others' backs and sigh with a mixture of relief and chagrin. "Why did we panic? What a lesson he taught us!"

Instead, Mark portrays the disciples as clueless as ever, still confused as to what had happened and with whom they were dealing. Their journey to faith was certainly not a smooth sea, but full of fits and starts and spills. That's good news for modern-day disciples who see no more clearly than the first twelve, but want to follow where Jesus leads.

>> BLESSED ASSURANCE

Disciples of every age may be comforted by this story's assurance that:

- we need not have a "watertight" theology or all our questions answered to trust in Jesus, just a willingness to "get in the boat."
- Jesus is present to support us in every wind storm of life (even when he appears to be asleep on the job or even nowhere to be found).
- if Jesus could put up with the confusion, questions, and doubts of those who witnessed his teaching and miracles up close and personal, he can surely put up with any confusion, questions, and doubts we may have.
- Jesus yearns for our trust in him to continually grow, but we need not pass any test or meet any standard to begin following where he leads.

»» WHAT ABOUT TODAY?

At home on the "information highway" and with a variety of social media, today's youth are uncomfortable with confusion and doubt but experience both nevertheless. The awareness that Jesus' own disciples were "experts" in these areas may reassure them that in matters of faith, it is willingness to embark on the journey, not absolute certainty, that matters most.

Less influenced by traditional value and belief systems than previous generations, many youth do not uncritically assume the Bible's authority. The Bible will have authority for them to the extent that it has specific relevance for the issues of their lives. Because this story addresses the universal human need to trust and depend on something in the midst of life's storms, it may have the appeal of relevance and the ring of authority for those seeking a trustworthy guide.

»» THE BOTTOM LINE

Now as then, the stilling of the storm is an appeal and challenge for disciples of every age to trust Jesus more, on whatever sea and in whatever weather we are sailing. Reassure participants that being a disciple of Jesus does not require spiritual certainty or fearless faith, but rather a simple, personal decision to follow where he leads.

In matters of faith, it is willingness to embark on the journey, not absolute certainty, that matters most.

Welcome to... Ambiguity!

Announcer: Welcome to the game show AMBIGUITY! And now, here's your host, Alex Reebok!

Host: Hello, and welcome once again to our game where the contestant who shows the most doubt and confusion wins! With our game, as you know, we provide the answers; you provide the questions. Now on to round 1. And the categories are: Geography, Generation X, Generation Y, Generation Z, and Biblical Characters. Contestant #1, you go first.

Contestant 1: I'll take Geography for $100, Alex.

Host: And the answer is: This northern continent contains the countries of Canada, the United States, and Mexico.

Contestant 2: *(excitedly raising hand)* What is North America?

Host: No, sorry. That's the *correct* answer.

Contestant 1: *(cautiously raising hand)* Could you repeat the answer?

Host: Yes! A brilliant display of confusion! Contestant #2, your turn.

Contestant 2: I'll take Biblical Characters for $100, Alex.

Host: And the answer is: A carpenter from Nazareth, this man once walked on water.

Contestant 2: *(confidently raising hand)* Who was Joseph?

Host: Judges?... I'm sorry, the judges say that's too nearly the *correct* answer, because Joseph was a relative.

Contestant 1: *(hesitantly raising hand)* He did *what???*

Host: A fine expression of doubt! Congratulations, Contestant #1. You've just won an all-expense paid trip to Lake Not-So-Sure, where the women are confused, the men are confounded, and the kids haven't got a clue!

DISCIPLE INGREDIENTS

(Excited observer) *Fewer doubts than the surest saint. More faithful than a farm dog. Able to leap tall questions in a single bound. Look! Up in the sky! It's a bird. It's a plane. It's SUPER DISCIPLE! Yes, it's SUPER DISCIPLE, who came to earth with certainty and confidence far beyond those of mortal believers and who, in his disguise as Clark Christian, fights a never-ending battle for truth, justice, and to promote his way as the only way!*

The media has always portrayed our cultural heroes, from Mother Teresa to LeBron James, as almost superhuman beings with few, if any, flaws. What qualities and characteristics do *you* think are really necessary to be a disciple, a follower of Jesus? List them below:

_____

_____

_____

Permission is granted to photocopy this handout for use with this session.

NOT YOUR EVERYDAY BOAT RIDE

Narrator:	"On that day, when evening had come, he said to them,"
Jesus:	"Let us go across to the other side."
Narrator:	"And leaving the crowd behind,"
Crowd:	That's us!
Narrator:	"they"
Disciples:	That's us!
Narrator:	"took him with them in the boat, just as he was."
Jesus:	How else would I go?
Narrator:	"Other boats were with him."
Crowd:	Must have been rush hour!
Narrator:	"A great windstorm arose, and the waves beat into the boat, so that the boat was already being swamped."
Crowd:	*(Make convincing windstorm noises.)*
Narrator:	"But he was in the stern, asleep on the cushion;"
Crowd:	Must have stayed up to watch Jimmy Fallon!
Narrator:	"and they woke him up"
Crowd:	Their first mistake!
Narrator:	"and said to him,"
Disciples:	"Teacher, do you not care that we are perishing?"
Crowd:	Their second mistake!
Narrator:	"He woke up"
Crowd:	Uh-oh!
Narrator:	"and rebuked the wind, and said to the sea,"
Jesus:	"Peace! Be still!"
Crowd:	And guess what?
Narrator:	"Then the wind ceased, and there was a dead calm."
Crowd:	We're talkin' total stillness here!
Narrator:	"He said to them,"
Crowd:	Here it comes….
Jesus:	"Why are you afraid? Have you still no faith?"
Crowd:	Not lookin' too good for the ol' doubting disciples here.
Narrator:	"And they were filled with great awe"
Crowd:	As you might expect.
Narrator:	"And said to one another,"
Crowd:	As you might *not* expect.
Disciples:	"Who then is this, that even the wind and the sea obey him?"
Crowd:	And you call these guys disciples???
Jesus:	Yes, any who try to follow where I lead.
Crowd:	But Jesus! They're so confused and unsure!
Jesus:	Like I said, any who try to follow where I lead!

Dear Jesus,
  when the wind is great,
  when the sea is high,
  when our boats are swamped,
  when our cries for help seem to go unheard, help us believe…
Dear Jesus,
  when our fear is great,
  when our confusion is high,
  when our doubts are pouring in,
  when our questions go unanswered, help us follow…
Dear Jesus,
  when the winds have died,
  when the sea has stilled,
  when our storm is over,
  help us see your love for us at work…
Dear Jesus,
  go with each one here into the time ahead,
  resting in the stern of our boats,
  *ready to calm **our** windstorms whenever we call. AMEN.*

Permission is granted to photocopy this handout for use with this session.

>>> **SESSION 2**

LEAVING OUR NETS >>>

>> **KEY VERSE**

And immediately they left their nets and followed him. (Mark 1:18)

>> **FAITH STORY**

Mark 1:16-20

>> **FAITH FOCUS**

Passing along the Sea of Galilee, Jesus abruptly called four ordinary fishermen to an extraordinary task—catching people into the realm of God! Just as abruptly, and with no apparent preparation or deliberation, they dropped everything to follow. (Are these guys *real*?)

>> **SESSION GOAL**

Guide participants to hear in this story that Jesus' call to discipleship includes them, and that following requires leaving the "nets" that tangle them up and tie them down.

>> **Materials needed and advance preparation**

- Contact someone to knock on the door or call on the phone (*Option A* in Focus).
- Writing paper
- Pencils/pens
- Chalkboard/chalk or newsprint/marker
- Bibles
- Copies of the handout sheet for Session 2
- Net bag or offering plate (Respond)

TEACHING PLAN

1. FOCUS 5-7 minutes

Distribute writing paper and pencils, and have participants number from 1-7. Then have them answer the following with the *first* thing that comes to their mind:

1. Write your name.
2. Name a location where you frequently hang out (could be in your house).
3. Write your first name again.
4. Write the name of a friend or a sibling.
5. Name something you and this person typically do together (like video gaming, riding horses, playing music).
6. Write a noun that is related to the above activity.
7. Name a piece of equipment that you use with the above activity.

Then ask them to fold their papers in half and pass them in. Inform them that you'll be using them later in the session. Then go on to one of the options below.

>> **Option A:** In advance, ask someone to knock on the meeting room door and repeatedly call for you, or have them call you on the cell phone but don't answer. Ignore the caller until he or she gives up, and in the meantime continue with the brief "Mad Lib" exercise above. Then go on to
Option A under Connect.

>> **Option B:** Write the word "CALL" on the chalkboard or newsprint and explain that one definition of "call" is "a summons or invitation." Now invite participants to remember a very important call they've received. Explain that the "call" could come in many forms (e.g., phone, text, social media, letter, e-mail, personal conversation, dream, sermon, song, "still small voice," etc.). Go on to **Option B** under Connect.

2. CONNECT 7-9 minutes

>> **Option A:** Now ask:

- *How did you feel when I ignored the person calling me?*
- *Did anyone feel anxious or tempted to answer it yourself?*
- *Why is it hard not to answer a ringing phone or text or knock on the door?*
- *What kind of calls or texts do you look forward to answering?*
- *What kind of calls or text do you prefer not answering?*
- *Have you ever gotten a call or text that really surprised or shocked you? How did it feel?*
- *The Bible shows God calling many people in many ways. Does God still call people today? If so, how?*
- *Have you ever received a "call" from God? If so, what was it like?*

>> **Option B:** Now ask:

- *In what form did your important call come?*
- *Would it have been as important if it had come in some other way?*
- *What made that particular call so important (e.g., who it was from, how it was made, when it came, etc.)?*
- *What made it different from other "calls" you've received?*
- *Have you ever gotten a call that really surprised or shocked you? How did it feel?*
- *The Bible shows God calling many people in many ways. Does God still call people today? If so, how?*
- *Have you ever received a "call" from God? If so, what was it like?*

3. EXPLORE THE BIBLE 15-17 minutes

Shift to this activity by saying: *If you think you've gotten some interesting calls, imagine being called "out of the blue" to drop whatever you're doing, leave everything behind, and begin a radically new life without even contacting home. It happened to four ordinary guys in the Bible. Let's see how they answered.*

Ask everyone to follow along in their Bibles as you read Mark 1:16-20. Then take the folded papers everyone handed in earlier. One by one, use the answers to fill in the outline on the handout sheet, in the style of a "Mad Lib." In so doing, you'll be reading aloud each person's individualized version of Mark 1:16-18. Some of these may turn out to be humorous, some poignant. As you finish each one, give the person their own handout sheet along with their answers, so they can fill in their own "Mad Lib" call sheet. Now ask:

- *If you had never seen Jesus before, how would you know he was for real? How did the disciples know?*
- *Would you drop everything and follow as the disciples did, or ask if you could "sleep on it"?*
- *How would it feel to really leave whatever you named in order to follow Jesus as the disciples left their nets?*
- *What would be the best thing about following him?*
- *What would be the hardest thing about following him?*

Conclude by making the following points:

- *Unlike a potential employer, Jesus doesn't examine our credentials, check our references, or wait until we graduate before inviting us to join his "company."*
- *He simply **calls** us out of whatever "boat" we happen to be in and says, "Follow me."*
- *When Jesus called Simon, Andrew, James, and John, they "immediately left their nets and followed him."*
- *We may want to follow Jesus, but usually prefer doing it on our own terms without "leaving our nets" or letting go of anything to do so.*

4. APPLY 9-11 minutes

>> **Option A:** Ask everyone to form a "human net" by standing in a circle, reaching out, and joining hands with someone across from them until every hand is firmly held by another. Tell them that you will be "Jesus" passing along the Sea of Galilee and they are the disciples holding onto their "nets." You will call them to follow you while walking around the room, and they must try to follow **without letting go** of their "nets." Now walk around the room in a random pattern, calling each participant by name (e.g., "Follow me, Susan," etc.) and watch as they struggle to do so. Now ask:

- *How did it **feel** to try to follow while holding on to your "nets"?*
- *Does this help you understand why the disciples had to leave **their** nets to follow Jesus?*
- *Can we truly follow Jesus without leaving **our** "nets"?*

Distribute pencils/pens and paper and ask everyone to write down three "nets" that tangle them up, tie them down, and discourage or distract them from answering Jesus' call. After a few moments, invite people to call out some of their "nets" and list them under the word NETS on a chalkboard or newsprint.

>> **Option B:** Distribute pencils/pens and paper and ask participants to write down the three things they value most in life. Ask them to fold or crumple the paper so they can hold it in a clenched fist. Divide the group into pairs and give each person 30 seconds to take their partner's piece of paper (i.e., their "most valued things") from them. Now ask:

- *How did it feel to have someone take (or try to take) your "most valued things" away?*
- *How did you try to protect and preserve your "most valued things"?*
- *Why is it so important for us to hold on to our most valued things?*
- *Can you imagine something for which you would **willingly** give up your most valued things?*
- *Could some of these things be the "nets" that tangle us up, tie us down, and discourage or distract us from answering Jesus' call?*
- *Can we truly follow Jesus without leaving our "nets"?*

Dear Jesus,

you know how hard it is to answer God's call—

because yours led to a cross.

You know how hard it is to leave "nets" behind—

because you were human too.

You know that when the call comes, the answer must be yes or no—

because there's no middle ground.

You know that in spite of the difficulties,

there is nothing more rewarding or fulfilling than answering God's call and following God's Way—

because you did.

Show us this Way, Jesus,

and accept the offering of our nets as a sign of our desire to untangle our lives from all that prevents us from fully answering your call.

Help us to do this so we may see you more clearly,

love you more dearly,

and follow you more nearly,

day by day. AMEN.

5. RESPOND 5-7 minutes

Explain that you will now take up an "Offering of Nets." Using the papers from Apply (they may have to uncrumple them!), ask everyone to write down the one "net" they most need to leave behind in order to answer Jesus' call and follow where he leads. When everyone is done, walk around with a net bag or offering plate and invite them to drop their "nets" in to signify their desire to untangle their lives and respond to Jesus' call. Conclude with the prayer in the sidebar (also on the bottom of the handout sheet) or one of your own choosing.

LOOK AHEAD

For next session, prepare slips of paper or "The Good Life Fast" pledge forms for whichever option you choose in Respond.

Also, if you will be using the Extender Session after Session 4, order the video. See Extender Session instructions for how to order.

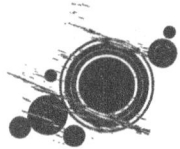

 # INSIGHTS FROM SCRIPTURE

"The time is fulfilled, and the kingdom of God has come near" (Mark 1:15a). With this incredible announcement, Jesus initiated his earthly ministry which began in a river and ended on a cross. In the time between, everything Jesus said and did proclaimed and made real the arrival of God's way of being, the reign of God's will "on *earth* as it is in *heaven*" (Matt. 6:10). Those who encountered the words and works of Jesus experienced the nearness of God, but in a *preliminary* way because the heavenly realm has yet to come in its fullness. Those who witnessed the teachings and miracles of Jesus experienced the reign of God, but in a *hidden* way because only those who had the "eyes of faith" could see it.

»» THE CALL

According to Lamar Williamson, the heart of discipleship in Mark's Gospel is, literally, to "come after" Jesus and bear witness to him in a world that desperately needs some good news. As soon as Jesus announced "the kingdom of God has come near," he called people to enter it by following him. And once called, it was decision time because there was little opportunity to deliberate. Nowhere is this clearer than in the seaside scene where Jesus abruptly appeared and called Simon, Andrew, James, and John without even a proper introduction. Jesus calls whom he will (mostly ordinary folk) with no regard for social status, income, or occupation, and he hopes for an immediate response.

»» THE RESPONSE

The absence of detail in this story frustrates our human need to understand the psychology of what's going on when people drop everything to follow a perfect stranger as the four fishermen did. Some scholars suggest there must have been prior contact with Jesus to prepare them for such an immediate and radical response, but nothing in the story suggests this. As Williamson points out, the lack of information brings focus to the Gospel's primary concern: the *authority* of Jesus who calls and the *response* of those who are called. According to Mark, this was their first encounter with Jesus and no previous contact explains the immediacy of their response. We are left with our mouths hanging open and our minds wondering if these people were sane. Could *we* do such a thing?

»» THE CATCH

There is, of course, a catch. As the first disciples demonstrate, following Jesus means to leave our "nets," to let go of all that tangles us up and ties us down to secure but unfulfilling lives. Like Abraham (Genesis 12:1), they left their family homes, an act that blatantly contradicted their cultural training and most basic self-interests. They also left their fishing occupation, steady work in those days, because fish was the main diet of the common people. But in so doing, they traded their livelihood for life and their human family for God's family.

There is another catch. Jesus said, "Follow me and I will make you fish for people" (Mark 1:17). Once called, disciples weren't to rest on their fishhooks (an uncomfortable image at best). They were to catch others into the coming reign of God, not with tackle and bait but with the incredible good news that in Jesus Christ, life with God has come near to *them*!

>> WHAT ABOUT TODAY?

Unlike earlier generations who enjoyed the superficial security of a tenuous Cold War stalemate and the Soviet suppression of ethnic hostilities, today's youth are seeing the "New World Order" dissolve into a downward spiral of violence and chaos. With so much uncertainty and instability all around, the prospect of committing one's life to following Jesus may seem both foolish (what if he's wrong?) *and* compelling (what if he's right?!).

Unlike earlier generations who had only Ten Commandments, today's youth were raised on an eleventh one as well: "Thou shalt not trust strangers." This deeply ingrained distrust of strangers may make the disciples' response to Jesus' call all the more puzzling. On the other hand, they may be all the more intrigued by the power and authority of a stranger who commands that kind of immediate trust.

In a changing world economy, youth are understandably concerned about their financial future. While they may feel compelled to work harder for financial security and cast nets wider in order to keep up, the alternative—getting out of that vicious cycle, leaving those nets behind, changing the game goals from accumulation of *more* to working for better— may have some real appeal. (For additional exploration of how we can move our economy in a more sustainable and just direction, see also Annie Leonard's *The Story of Solutions*, http://storyofstuff.org/movies/the-story-of-solutions/.)

>> THE BOTTOM LINE

At the heart of the matter, Jesus' call to follow is a challenge to examine one's ultimate loyalties in life and where they will be invested. This simple, compelling story speaks to those who are searching for more than climbing ladders as well as to those whose discipleship has degenerated into attending mass and filling personal "nets" the rest of the week.

Unlike earlier generations who had only Ten Commandments, today's youth were raised on an eleventh one as well: "Thou shalt not trust strangers."

Yet disciples are called to trade their livelihood for life and their human family for God's family.

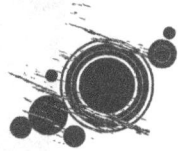

Called by Name

In Real Life
Exploring tough questions facing youth today

_____'s
_____ (your name)
(ever so slightly)
REVISED VERSION OF MARK 1:16-18

As Jesus passed along _____, he saw
(a location where you hang out)

_____ and _____ _____ (activity you typically
(your name)   (a sibling or friend's name)

_____—for they were _____.
do together)   (a noun related to above activity)

And Jesus said, "Follow me and I will make you fish for people." And
IMMEDIATELY they **LEFT** their _____ and **FOLLOWED** him.
(a piece of equipment used with above activity)

Clueless and Called : Session 2

>>>
Dear Jesus,
   you know how hard it is to answer God's call—because yours led to a cross.
You know how hard it is to leave "nets" behind—because you were human too.
You know that when the call comes, the answer must be yes or no—because there's no middle ground.
You know that in spite of the difficulties, there is nothing more rewarding or fulfilling than answering God's call
   and following God's Way—because you did.
Show us this Way, Jesus,
   and accept the offering of our nets as a sign of our desire to untangle our lives
   from all that prevents us from fully answering your call.
Help us to do this so we may see you more clearly,
   love you more dearly, and follow you more nearly, day by day. AMEN.

Permission is granted to photocopy this handout for use with this session.

>>> **SESSION 3**

GETTING TO 'THE GOOD LIFE' >>>

>> KEY VERSE

"For those who want to save their life will lose it, and those who lose their life for my sake, and for the sake of the gospel, will save it." (Mark 8:35)

>> FAITH STORY

Mark 8:31-37

>> FAITH FOCUS

After rebuking Peter for tempting him to save his life rather than fulfill his mission, Jesus said in no uncertain terms that following him meant self-denial. He clued the disciples in to a baffling paradox: It is in losing one's life for the sake of Jesus and the good news that real life is truly found.

>> SESSION GOAL

Help participants understand that the truly "good life," life with meaning, purpose, and fulfillment, is not found in self-promotion but in self-denial for the sake of Jesus and God's reign.

>> Materials needed and advance preparation

- Pencils/pens
- Writing paper
- Chalkboard/chalk or newsprint/marker
- Bibles
- Copies of the first handout sheet for Session 3 (Explore)
- Small slips of paper (*Option B* in Apply)
- "The Good Life Fast" pledge forms and envelopes (*Option A* in Respond)

TEACHING PLAN

1. FOCUS 6-8 MINUTES

>> **Option A:** Ask everyone to close their eyes, relax, and visualize the following:

Walking along a road one day, you see a crumpled beer can and pick it up to recycle the aluminum.

Rubbing off the dirt, you're puzzled to see that it's called "Big Genie Beer," a brand you've never heard of.

Suddenly, a column of smoke rises out of the can and turns into what appears to be... a big genie!

Thanking you for releasing her after years in the can, the genie says she will grant you one wish.

When you ask about the other two, she explains that the "United Genie Union" now allows only one wish because so many genies were suffering from GPC (Genie Physical Collapse) after trying to grant three.

Wavering between being ruler of the universe and passing your next math test, you finally wish for the genie to give you "the good life." The genie agrees but says she's not sure what "the good life" is.

Now distribute pencils/pens and paper to everyone. Tell them their assignment is to describe their version of "the good life" for the genie by listing five of its most basic ingredients. Then go on to **Option A** under Connect.

 Option B: Ask participants to place themselves on a "human continuum." Designate one end of the room as "Strongly Disagree" and the other end "Strongly Agree." Then have them move on the continuum to show their response to each of the answers provided. Ask:

*Which of the following represents "the good life" in our **society** today?*

1. Driving the best car
2. Intentionally living on less to give more away
3. Making a lot of money
4. Having a great vegetable garden
5. Wearing the latest fashions
6. Being sexually active
7. Having the best electronics and technology
8. Serving in the armed forces
9. Volunteering in a soup kitchen or shelter for the homeless
10. Going to church regularly

Now continue with **Option B** under Connect.

2. CONNECT 7-9 minutes

>> **Option A:** Ask each person to name two or three of the five ingredients on their list and write them under the heading INGREDIENTS OF THE GOOD LIFE on a chalkboard or piece of newsprint. Now ask:

- *What do these ingredients say about how **you** define "the good life"?*
- *Are these the same ingredients that our **society** would include in "the good life"?*
- *According to society, what must one **have** or **do** to attain "the good life"?*
- *Have you experienced "the good life" most when serving yourself or serving others? Why?*

>> **Option B:** Now ask:

- *What do your responses say about how **society** defines "the good life"?*
- *Are these the same things **you** believe represent "the good life"?*
- *According to society, what must one **have** or **do** to attain the "good life"?*
- *Which of the behaviors didn't seem to fit in to society's definition of "the good life"? Why?*
- *Have you experienced "the good life" most when serving yourself or serving others? Why?*

3. EXPLORE THE BIBLE 10 minutes

Shift to this activity by saying: *If it's not so easy to define "the good life," there may be good reason for it. Let's turn to the Gospel of Mark and see what Jesus has to say about "the good life" and how we get to it.*

Invite everyone to turn to Mark 8:31-38 in their Bibles. Ask for two volunteers to read, having one be the narrator and the other be the voice of Jesus.

>>>
Today, many youth are seeing that consumerism has its limits and are asking if there's more to life. The invitation of Jesus to deny oneself may at first put off those so accustomed to putting things on. But they'll appreciate his straightforward style and his willingness to do what so few advertisers dare: tell the truth.

Now read aloud "The Tale of Telemachus" on the first handout sheet. Invite everyone to listen carefully for connections between the tale of Telemachus and the teaching of Jesus in the Bible passage just read.

After reading it out loud, lead a discussion with the following questions:

- *Jesus said, "If any want to become my followers, let them deny themselves and take up their cross and follow me" (Mark 8:34). How did Telemachus "take up his cross" and follow Jesus at first? Later?*
- *Jesus said, "Those who lose their life for my sake, and for the sake of the gospel, will save it" (Mark 8:35b). In what way did Telemachus "save" his life by losing it? What other lives were saved through Telemachus losing his own?*
- *Can you think of people who have "saved" their lives, or the lives of others, by sacrificing "the good life" as society defines it?* (Be prepared to suggest several, such as St. Francis, Mother Teresa, Martin Luther King Jr., Oscar Romero (https://www.franciscanmedia.org/saint-oscar-arnulfo-romero/), Rachel Corrie (http://rachelcorriefoundation.org/rachel), Jean Donovan (http://www.uscatholic.org/culture/war-and-peace/2010/12/even-unto-death-martyrdom-jean-donovan), Tom Fox (http://en.wikipedia.org/wiki/Tom_Fox_%28Quaker%29), a parent, a teacher, et al).

4. APPLY 12 minutes

>> **Option A:** **(for smaller groups or retreat setting):** Take everyone on a quick trip to the local donut shop or icecream place. Before you leave, take inventory to see how much money you have among the group members. If few people have money, give each person a couple of dollars to spend. When you arrive at the shop, give everyone a chance to choose what they want to buy, but step in just before they actually get to the counter to make their purchase. Ask if they are willing to give up what they were about to order and give you the money instead, to be used for the local food pantry. You might very well leave without eating or drinking!

Even if some or all people decide to go ahead and order, you will have lots of discussion possibilities about "denying oneself." If you collected money, give one or two of the participants responsibility for getting the money to the food pantry or to the church collection. Follow up your trip by discussing:

- *Did you miss what you gave up more or less than you thought you would? Why?*
- *What does **your** story have to do with the tale of Telemachus or the teaching of Jesus about losing our lives to save them?*

Go on to **Option A** in Respond below.

>> **Option B:** Have everyone think of some item they *most* would like to buy right now. Tell everyone to raise their hands if they have the money to get it immediately. If any don't have the money, ask: *Where would you get the money? Save it? Work for it? Ask parents? How long would it take for you to get it?* After you've established a way for people to get the item they want, distribute slips of paper and pencils. On the paper, have everyone write down their own name and the name of the item.

Go on to **Option B** in Respond below.

5. RESPOND 7 minutes

>> **Option A:** Ask everyone to practice "denying themselves" by choosing one of the following things that they feel would be hardest for them to give up, or something that most prevents them from taking up their cross and experiencing "the good life" God intends for all:

- Phone
- Video games
- A *specific* junk food
- Any special purchases
- Alcohol/drugs
- A particular relationship that is not good for them, etc.

Give everyone an envelope to go with the pledge form on the second handout sheet, "The Good Life Fast."

Suggest that they fast for one to two weeks (depending on the type of fast). Have them seal the pledge form in the envelope, and take it home with them from your meeting.

Set up support with periodic phone calling or other social media from peers during their simultaneous fast. Make clear that fasting is not simply about denying oneself, but a way to help focus on and deepen relationship with God and neighbors by reducing distractions.

Conclude by praying together "The Prayer of Saint Francis" on the first handout sheet.

>> **Option B:** As a way of practicing "denying" themselves, ask people to mark their slips of paper with a **Y** if they are *willing **not** to buy that item* for at least six months. It might mean that they no longer want it after that time. Invite them to make plans, as a group, to pool and spend the money they would have spent, perhaps on grocery shopping together for the local food pantry (or choose another way to donate). Have everyone turn in their slips of paper to you.

Conclude by praying together the "Prayer of Saint Francis" on the first handout sheet.

LOOK AHEAD

For Session 5, contact a parishioner for the baptism interview (*Option A* in Focus).

INSIGHTS FROM SCRIPTURE

Mark 8:27–9:1 defines the Way of Jesus. The passage therefore also defines the way of his followers. In a few short verses, it moves us from who Jesus is (vss. 27-30) to what being the Messiah means (vss. 31-33) to what following the Messiah requires (vss. 34-37).

> For those who truly take up their cross and follow, "getting to the good life" may look to society like getting nowhere at all.

›› WHAT MESSIAH MEANS

In ancient Israel, the word Messiah literally meant "anointed" and referred to the practice of anointing and thus consecrating people for special offices or tasks, such as those of prophet, priest, or king.

Looking back, the people remembered the glorious days of King David's rule as the greatest period in their history and believed that an anointed descendent of David would always rule their kingdom. But after the fall of the nation in 586 B.C.E, they came to believe that the Messiah would be a descendent of David who would at some time in the future crash into history, utterly destroy their enemies, and reestablish a political Davidic kingdom that would rule the world forever.

With the expectation of this kind of Davidic Messiah widespread in Jesus' day, it is little wonder that Peter rebuked Jesus for saying that as Messiah he must suffer, be rejected, and be killed (8:31). Suffering and death were to be inflicted *by* the Messiah, not *upon* the Messiah!

Rather than gently correct Peter's misconception, Jesus ordered, "Get behind me, Satan!" (8:33a) because Peter's assertion was tempting him to believe he might yet avoid the suffering, rejection, and death that lay ahead. For Jesus, as for us, the urge to survive was strong. The well-intentioned words of his friend Peter were a temptation of the most personal kind.

›› WHAT FOLLOWING THE MESSIAH REQUIRES

Having declared that Peter's perspective was all too human (8:33b), Jesus laid out the divine perspective on what it means to follow a radically different kind of Messiah.

First, it meant denying oneself. The Greek word for "deny" is the same as that used in Peter's denial of Jesus in 14:72 where Peter in essence "disowns" him. Thus to deny oneself is to disown oneself, to give up all selfish pretensions and earthly securities for the sake of following the Messiah. It is not simply a call to deny oneself some *thing*. Neither is it a call to reject or hate oneself, as if the God of love would ever desire that. To deny oneself, as Bible scholar Lamar Williamson points out, is to acknowledge that we can never "possess" our own lives and can only find our true meaning, purpose, and fulfillment in offering our lives to the Messiah and others. This denial of self is what the cross is really all about.

›› NOTHING TO LOSE

Jesus offers a perplexing paradox that turns all our human wisdom on its head. "For those who want to save their life will lose it, and those who lose their life for my sake, and for the sake of the gospel, will save it" (8:35). Society teaches we must save, accumulate, and acquire to experience the "good life." Jesus teaches that we must lose, deny, and disown to experience God's "good life." It is precisely when we have nothing to lose that we have everything to gain. It is only as we are emptied of distractions that we may be filled with all that God yearns to give.

›› WHAT ABOUT TODAY?

Today's youth have their own favorite brands and enjoy the pleasures that pop culture provides. At the same time, many are seeing that consumerism has its limits and are asking if there's more to life. The invitation of Jesus to deny oneself may at first *put off* those so accustomed to *putting things on*. But they'll appreciate his straightforward style and his willingness to do what so few advertisers dare: *tell the truth*.

More open to defining "the good life" in emotional and spiritual rather than purely material terms, youth may be intrigued at the prospect of "getting to it" by following an unorthodox Messiah rather than an impersonal stock market. Impatient with business as usual, they may find Jesus' invitation to take up his cross a refreshing alternative to society's invitation to climb up its ladder.

Finally, youth are suspicious of a popular Christianity that looks too much like the culture it professes to be *in* but not *of*. Their concern for truth in advertising applies to issues of faith as well. With so many Christians and congregations appearing to "climb the ladder" they condemn rather than "carry the cross" they proclaim, there is reason to be concerned. Honestly acknowledging the church's failure to "carry its cross" and reminding youth of their opportunity to help the church "pick it back up" may be for some an appealing challenge.

›› THE BOTTOM LINE

Because Jesus was a radically different kind of Messiah, following him requires a radically different worldview in which self-fulfillment is found through self-denial, not self-promotion. For those who truly take up their cross and follow, "getting to the good life" may look to society like getting nowhere at all.

THE TALE OF TELEMACHUS

Exploring tough questions facing youth today

Clueless and Called : Session 3

There once lived a monk named Telemachus who decided to live in the desert alone and devote his life to God, so that he would save his soul. Then Telemachus realized that to truly love and serve God, he must leave the desert and go to Rome where he could love and serve God's children.

By this time, Christianity was the official religion of Rome and yet there were still the Roman arenas where gladiators killed each other to entertain the "Christian" citizens. When Telemachus arrived at the arena and saw men for whom Christ died about to be killed for sport, he was appalled. Still in his hermit's robes, he leapt into the arena and stood between the gladiators. Pushed out of the way, he again placed himself between them. Irritated by the interruption, the crowd yelled for the gladiators to kill him so the games could go on. At the commander's order, a gladiator struck Telemachus with his sword and he lay dead on the ground.

Shocked that a monk had been killed in this way, the crowd suddenly realized the horror of what they had been watching. The gladiator games ended in Rome that day, never to begin again.

(paraphrased from William Barclay's *The Gospel of Mark*)

The Prayer of Saint Francis

*Lord, make me an instrument
   of your peace.*

*Where there is hatred…
   let me sow love.*

Where there is injury…pardon.

Where there is doubt…faith.

Where there is despair…hope.

Where there is darkness…light.

Where there is sadness…joy.

*O Divine Master,
   grant that I may not so much seek*

To be consoled…as to console,

To be understood…as to understand,

*To be loved…as to love,
   for*

It is in giving…that we receive,

*It is in pardoning…
   that we are pardoned,*

*It is in dying…
   that we are born to eternal life.*

Permission is granted to photocopy this handout for use with this session.

THE GOOD LIFE FAST

In Real Life
Exploring tough questions facing youth today

To find out what it means to "deny myself" and more fully experience "the good life" God intends for me, I pledge to fast from

_____ for _____
(thing or behavior)   (length of time)

This FAST will begin on _____
                          (date and time)

and end on _____
             (date and time)

Signed: _____ Date: _____

>>>

Fasting is not simply about denying yourself, but a way to help focus on and deepen relationship with God and neighbors by reducing distractions. Anytime you notice you are longing for what you are fasting from, turn it into a prayer for a closer walk with God.

Clueless and Called : Session 3

Permission is granted to photocopy this handout for use with this session.

>>> **SESSION 4**

TRAVELING LIGHT >>>

>> KEY VERSES

He ordered them to take nothing for their journey except a staff; no bread, no bag, no money in their belts; but to wear sandals and not to put on two tunics. (Mark 6:8-9)

>> FAITH STORY

Mark 6:6b-13

>> FAITH FOCUS

Leaving Galilee and returning to his hometown of Nazareth, Jesus taught in the synagogue, only to be treated with suspicion and contempt by people who were offended by his presumption. To supplement his own teaching, Jesus called the twelve disciples, gave them full authority to carry on his mission, and sent them out by twos. In so doing, he ordered them to take only the barest necessities to ensure their radical dependence on God.

>> SESSION GOAL

Help participants see that a radical trust in God brings with it freedom from the vicious cycle of competition, popularity, and success, and freedom for the deepest love, joy, and meaning life can offer.

>> Materials needed and advance preparation

- Media player; Internet access (*Option A* in Focus)
- Scraps of paper to scatter around the room (*Option C* in Focus)
- Copies of the handout sheet for Session 4
- Bibles
- Pencils/pens
- Writing paper
- Chalkboard/chalk or newsprint/marker

TEACHING PLAN

1. FOCUS 7 minutes

>> **Option A:** Tell the following story, or watch the YouTube video (https://youtu.be/vTqLmFS4yDs):

Ted Studebaker grew up on a farm in Ohio. In high school, he played football, ran track, wrestled, and was recognized by his classmates as the senior boy having achieved the most. A young man of faith, Ted was opposed to all war and registered as a conscientious objector during the Vietnam War. After graduating from college and graduate school, Ted volunteered to go to Vietnam, not to fight, but to help the Vietnamese improve their farming methods. During his second year there, he married Ven Pak, a Chinese woman who was also a volunteer. Ted worked in the Di Linh area where many had been killed during the war. He knew his life was in danger, but he chose to stay. Ted was shot to death just a week after his wedding.

Before his death, Ted wrote in a letter to his family and friends back home: "Above all, Christ taught me how to love all people, including enemies, and to return good for evil."
(adapted from *Ted Studebaker: A Man Who Loved Peace*, by Joy Hofacker Moore)

Go on to **Option A** under Connect.

>> **Option B:** Tell the following story:

Perhaps you heard about the mountain climber who was nearly to the top of a high peak when suddenly her rope broke and she began falling toward her death on the rocks far below. Frantically reaching out, her hand brushed against something and she grabbed hold of a tree root that had grown out of the mountainside. Dangling there between heaven and earth, she knew it was just a matter of time before she would lose her grip.

Just when she had given up all hope, she heard some rumbling from up above and shouted out in desperation, "Is anybody up there?" After what seems like an eternal pause, a voice replied, "Yes. It's the Lord."

Never having been particularly religious, she decided that, given the circumstances, it was worth a try. "Lord," she yelled back, "can you help me?" After another pause, there came this reply, "Yes, but *only* if you let go of the root." Thinking the thin mountain air must have affected her brain, she shouted back, "What did you say?" Again came the response, "*Only* if you let go of the root."

Looking up to the heavens above and then down at the rocks below, she shouted with all her might, "Is anybody *else* up there?"

Go on to **Option B** under Connect.

>> **Option C:** In advance, tear up some papers into bits, enough to make a pretty big mess in your meeting area. On one or two of them, write "Trust God." Then scatter the bits all over the room. When participants come in, instruct them to look for the bits of paper with the "trust God" message on them, and to throw the rest into the trash. Make the point that if there had been only a few pieces of extra paper around, it would have been easy to find the message pieces. Carry the point to an analogy: If we have too much "stuff," it's harder to find the thing we really need or want.

Follow up with the questions under **Option C** in Connect.

2. CONNECT 7 minutes

>> **Option A:** Now lead a discussion with the following questions:

- *Ted was a talented young man with a bright future. Why did he risk his life in Vietnam?*
- *Ted trusted God so much that he left his family behind and gave up many comforts to serve in Vietnam. Have there ever been times in **your** life when trusting God meant letting go of or giving up something important?*
- *Ted gave his time, and ultimately his life, following the example of Jesus' love. If we give up something important to follow Jesus, is there anything we get in return?*

>> **Option B:** Now lead a discussion with the following questions:

- *What do you think is the point of this story?* (trusting God)
- *At what point did the mountain climber decide not to trust God with her life?* (when God asked her to demonstrate that trust by letting go of the root)

TOUGH QUESTIONS:

- Why is there so much anxiety, emptiness, and pain for so many who "have it all"?
- If I buy into this "God thing" what's in it for me?
- If trusting God for everything is so great, why aren't more Christians out there doing it?

- *Have there ever been times in your life when trusting God meant letting go of or giving up something secure?*
- *Put yourself in the mountain climber's boots. What do you think you would have done?*

>> **Option C:** Now ask:

- *Have you ever had trouble finding something you needed because you had to search through lots of junk first?*

(Solicit brief stories from participants; perhaps they couldn't find something because their closet or drawers or lockers were a mess. You might even get more in-depth accounts involving searching for identities, self-confidence, etc.)

- *Have you ever decided to "clean house" and get rid of all the junk? How did you feel before you started? When you finished? Were you better able to work? To think? To concentrate?*

Tell this cautionary tale: *One way to capture small monkeys is to place a treat in a hollowed out coconut shell secured to a tree. The opening is just large enough for a small monkey hand to reach in and grab the treat, but too small for the clenched fist to draw back out again. Unless the monkey lets go of the treat, it's caught.*

3. EXPLORE THE BIBLE 12-14 minutes

Shift to this activity by saying: *Getting down to what's really important, and trusting God for what you need, is tough. Imagine being sent on a difficult mission with nothing but the shirt on your back, the shoes on your feet, and a staff in your hand. This actually happened to those twelve guys Jesus called disciples. Let's take a look.*

Distribute the handout sheets and divide into groups of two, three, or four. Explain that each group is to read Mark 6:7-13, answer the questions under "Traveling Light," and have one member report back to the whole group.

After 8-10 minutes, ask each group to report their findings. Use information from the Insights from Scripture section to suggest appropriate responses.

4. APPLY 11-13 minutes

>> **Option A:** Invite participants to follow along as you read "Changing Directions" (on the handout sheet) and then discuss some or all of the following questions:

- *Were the Fullers crazy to give away all they had and start over?*
- *Could they have started Habitat for Humanity without radically trusting God and letting go of their fortune? Do you think they would have?*
- *How do you respond to Linda Fuller's statement that the more she got, the more she wanted?*
- *Why didn't she feel fulfilled?*
- *What does Jesus' command for his disciples to "travel light" on their journey have to do with Millard and Linda Fuller's journey? With **our** journey?*
- *How could "traveling light" and trusting God to provide what we really need help us break out of the cycle of competition, popularity, and success?*

>> **Option B:** Some cultures have regular community celebrations or rites of passage in which people give away objects precious to them. It is a way of acknowledging that our worth does not lie in possessions, as well as being a personal discipline.

Challenge each other in your group to a "giveaway." Use this Apply time to EXPLAIN THE CONCEPT AND SET UP A TIME FOR THE CELEBRATION, preferably within a week or two of this session. To start off, ask everyone to imagine someone robbing their home, or imagine that their home burned down (no one was hurt). What object(s) would they feel saddest to lose? After a few moments, say: *Now that you've thought about what's very valuable to you, think about **voluntarily** giving that something away. What might it be?* Then suggest the idea of a giveaway. Make the following points:

- Participation is not mandatory. (But challenge everyone to try it.) Everyone is welcome at the celebration whether or not they participate in the actual giveaway.
- Each person participating should take time to think carefully about what they would give away. It could be something that distracts them from their relationship with God, or something that is a real challenge for them to part with. Either way, it will mean more if the thing they choose cannot easily be replaced (**NOT** "I was going to get a new one next month anyway").
- Anyone who participates will not be doing so *alone*. Like Jesus sending the disciples out by twos, so there is companionship in the giveaway.
- The giveaway is not just an exercise. You will not get your own possessions back. You may end up with something similar, but don't expect it.

Make the actual giveaway a time of celebration, of freeing each other up to better serve God, and of the challenge of maturity that the giveaway represents. Have people wrap the giveaway items ahead of time, and choose a way (drawing numbers or letters) to distribute the items. Here are some questions to ask either before or after the actual giveaway celebration:

- *Describe your feelings.*
- *What do you hope to gain from this experience? (Do you think you might get someone else's better stuff?)*
- *What happens in our group if someone gives away something very valuable and gets something of much less monetary worth?*
- *Would it make a difference in your feelings about the giveaway if your things went to someone you didn't know, or to a relief agency?*

(You might also ask anyone who chose not to participate to say how they felt, if you feel it would not put them too much on the spot.)

5. RESPOND 7-9 minutes

Distribute pencils/pens and paper to everyone. Invite them to imagine that Jesus has given them authority, sent them out, and ordered them to take nothing for their journey except the clothes on their back, the shoes on their feet, and two other things. Ask them to write down these two other things. After a few moments, ask each of them to name the things they would take on their journey and list them on a chalkboard or newsprint under the heading NOTHING ON MY JOURNEY WITH JESUS EXCEPT... Now ask:

- *Why did you choose to take along the things you did?*
- *If you were able to travel this "lightly" through life, what difference would it make in your perspectives, relationships, and priorities?*
- *Could "traveling light" ever mean leaving your family obligations behind?*

Now invite people to imagine trusting God for all their needs so completely on this journey that they are free to focus on the two things that really matter most. Ask them to write down these two things. After a few moments, ask each person to name the things that matter most and list them on the chalkboard or newsprint under the heading TRUSTING GOD FOR ALL THINGS, I'M FREE TO FOCUS ON... Now ask:

- *Why did you choose to focus on the things you did?*
- *What are some other benefits of trusting God to provide what we really need?*
- *Why might it be important to travel with others (i.e., "two by two") on this journey rather than alone?*

Make the point that:

Jesus might ask you to give up what you have, but *you won't be alone!* (Jesus purposely sent the disciples out in twos.)

Conclude by praying the following prayer or one in your own words:

Dear Jesus,
you have called us,
given us authority,
and sent us out to continue the ministry that you began.
You have ordered us to travel light on this journey
because you know we are easily distracted by so many things.
Help us know what to take and what to leave behind.
Open our eyes to the example and companionship of others who are "traveling light."
Help us trust you so completely
that we are free to focus on what matters most and
experience the deepest love, joy, and meaning life has to offer. AMEN.

LOOK AHEAD

The next session would be a good time for the Extender Session, "The Healing River," if you planned to incorporate it into the study. If not, confirm plans with a parishioner for the baptism interview (Session 5: Focus, Option A).

INSIGHTS FROM SCRIPTURE

Given the disciples' track record so far, one might question Jesus' wisdom in continuing to use such flawed instruments for so important an operation. But Jesus requires obedience, not perfection. He sent them out (almost in spite of themselves) to change the world.

›› TWO BY TWO (AND CHRIST-POWERED)

Lamar Williamson points out that even though Jesus could have covered more ground sending them out individually, he sent the disciples out two by two to provide support for each other, validate their witness, and show that even on the road, they belonged to a community of faith. While the decision to follow Jesus is profoundly individual, everything else about the Christian faith, from worship to Bible study to mission, is profoundly communal (according to the model Jesus and his disciples provided).

Like the first disciples, we are sent out to continue and extend the ministry of Jesus. But we cannot accomplish this mission by the power of our own resources or the authority of our own lives. *And we're not supposed to!* When we go out in obedience, the authority and power of Christ operates *through* us. As Lamar Williamson puts it, "That is why he dares to send us, why we dare to go, and why remarkable good still comes through the obedience of inadequate messengers."

›› SHAKING OFF DUST

Jesus' stern order for the disciples to "shake off the dust" on their feet reflected the practice of strict Jews who shook the dust from their feet when returning to Palestine from another country. It signified that a Jew could not have fellowship with even the dust of Gentile (non-Jewish) lands. For the disciples, shaking off the dust was a testimony against those who would not welcome or hear them. In this context, the act probably signified that once they had done all they could to proclaim the good news, the rest was between their hearers and God. Their mission was to obey Jesus' command, not assume responsibility for how others responded.

>> TRAVELING LIGHT

In sending them out, Jesus was no travel agent suggesting what they should pack. He was the Son of God ordering "them to take nothing for their journey except" a traveler's staff, the sandals on their feet, and the garment on their back (6:8-9). Jesus knew how preoccupation with physical comfort and material resources could distract them from their mission (as it distracts us from ours). To ensure their radical dependence on God, he allowed only the barest necessities on the journey.

This reliance on God enabled the disciples (and enables us) to strip away all that distracts and to focus on what matters most: continuing and extending Jesus' healing ministry in the world. When we align with God's way of being, we no longer need to fit in with the crowd. When we're unconditionally accepted by God, we no longer need to strive for the acceptance of others. When we're assured of having our real needs met, we are fulfilled without the "needs" our society creates. This is not simplicity rooted in religious obligation, but a simplicity born of trust that God will provide!

>> WHAT ABOUT TODAY?

Today's youth are influenced by advertising and consumerism, but are also wondering if products really deliver on the excitement, pleasure, and peace they promise. They don't have to look far to see the anxiety, emptiness, and pain of many who "have it all." Trusting God and "traveling light" may be attractive to those who are getting fed up with all the commercial hype.

People are naturally concerned with what's in it for them if they trade the promises of popular culture for the challenge—and promise—of the realm of God. The idea of being radically free from the intense social pressures they feel every day may have real appeal for those seeking a meaningful alternative.

Some youth will be skeptical about the benefits of trusting God for everything because there seem to be so few Christians out there really doing it. While extraordinary examples may be few, youth should be reminded that there are many thousands of disciples quietly trusting God and continuing the ministry of Jesus every day.

>> THE BOTTOM LINE

Jesus' charge to "travel light" on our journey of discipleship is both demand and promise. It demands that we trust God completely to provide all our needs, and promises that such trust will bring freedom for what matters most.

Traveling Light
Mark 6:7-13

In Real Life
Exploring tough questions facing youth today

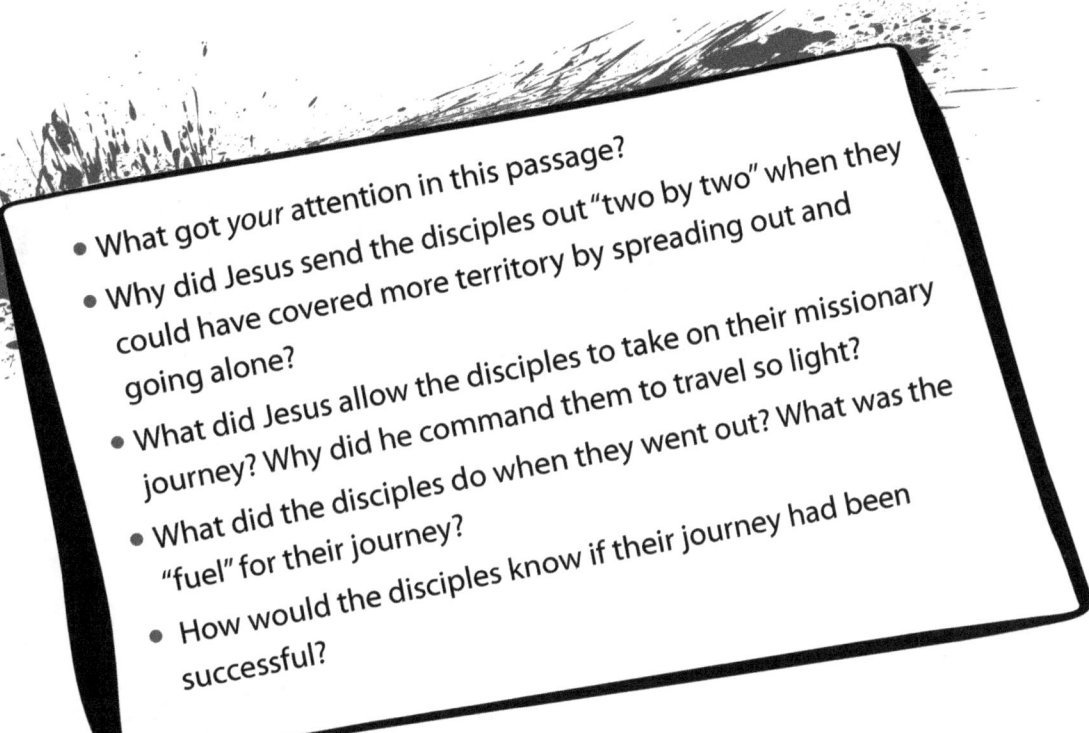

- What got your attention in this passage?
- Why did Jesus send the disciples out "two by two" when they could have covered more territory by spreading out and going alone?
- What did Jesus allow the disciples to take on their missionary journey? Why did he command them to travel so light?
- What did the disciples do when they went out? What was the "fuel" for their journey?
- How would the disciples know if their journey had been successful?

Changing Directions

By the age of 30, Millard Fuller had made his first million and had a goal of making 9 million more. During a crisis in their marriage relationship, he and his wife, Linda, decided to sell their business along with everything they had, give the money away, and start fresh—this time with God in charge. From there they founded Habitat for Humanity, an ecumenical Christian housing ministry that seeks to eliminate poverty housing from the world. Habitat affiliates build and sell houses to people in need at no profit and with no interest charged.

As Linda Fuller later reflected, "We had almost everything money could buy.... But I began to realize that the more I got, the more I wanted. And I didn't feel fulfilled. I felt like I was living contrary to [what] I was reading in the Bible."

(Diane McDougall, "There's No Place Like Home," *Worldwide Challenge Magazine*)

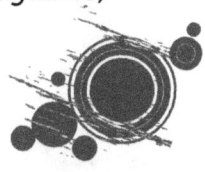

Permission is granted to photocopy this handout for use with this session.

>>> **SESSION 5**

MORE THAN GETTING WET >>>

>> KEY VERSE

In those days Jesus came from Nazareth of Galilee and was baptized by John in the Jordan. (Mark 1:9)

>> FAITH STORY

Mark 1:1-11

>> FAITH FOCUS

In fulfillment of ancient prophecy, John the baptizer came to prepare the way for Jesus, the one he declared would baptize "with the Holy Spirit" (1:8). Jesus then came down from Galilee and submitted to John's baptism in the Jordan River, establishing his identity as God's Beloved Son. The appearance of the dove at Jesus' baptism signified that the Spirit-famine was ended, the prophesies were fulfilled, and that God's Spirit was alive and at work in the ministry of Jesus.

>> SESSION GOAL

Help participants identify and claim baptism as the beginning of a faith identity and discipleship that requires genuine repentance and commitment, not moral perfection.

>> Materials needed and advance preparation

- Contact a parishioner for the baptism interview and go over the interview questions and thrust of the session (*Option A* in Focus).
- Copies of the handout sheet for Session 5
- Pens/pencils
- Bibles
- Chalkboard/chalk or newsprint/marker
- Washable markers
- Basin with water, towel, soap

TEACHING PLAN

1. FOCUS 8-10 minutes

>> **Option A:** *Briefly* interview a parishioner who recently went through the RCIA process and received the sacraments of initiation, including baptism. Another option is to interview someone who recently became a godparent of an infant who was baptized. It should be someone the youth respect. Be sure the interviewee understands her/his responses should be brief and to the point. Use the following questions as a guide:

(for an adult who was recently baptized)

- Why did you enter the RCIA process? What made you choose baptism? (sometimes the answers to these two questions can be different, as in the case of someone who joins RCIA because their future spouse is Catholic, and ends up receiving the sacraments because of a genuine conversion experience.)

- *How did you know when you were ready to be baptized?*
- *Why did you "go public" with your decision to follow Jesus by being baptized rather than just make a personal commitment?*
- *Since baptism involves dying to the old life and rising to new life in Christ, have you avoided failing ever since?*
- *I've heard that baptism is also a baptism into ministry, but I thought our priest was the minister. Do you have a ministry in the church?*
- *Some people declare that relationship with God and Jesus is a very personal thing. Does participation in the faith community really matter?*

(for a godparent)

- *What was your reaction when you were approached to be a godparent?*
- *What personal meaning does being a godparent have for you? What special responsibilities do you have as a godparent?*
- *How does being a godparent affect your life as a follower of Jesus?*
- *Do you have to lead a morally perfect life in order to be a godparent?*

Youth ask...

- What if I want to follow Jesus but not get mixed up with a church that seems more concerned with religious appearance than genuine commitment?
- If relationship with God is such a personal thing, why should I bother with baptism and church membership?
- Why do some Christians say baptism is only for adults, but Catholics baptize infants?

>> **Option B:** Ask participants to place themselves on a continuum as they respond to the following statements. Identify one end of the room as "Strongly Agree" and the other end as "Strongly Disagree."

- Since God knows when we're following Jesus, baptism isn't really necessary.
- Since baptism involves dying to the old life and rising to new life in Christ, we can never fall again after we're baptized.
- The most important thing is having faith. Baptism is just for show.
- Every baptized member of the church is just as much a minister as our priest(s).
- Since my relationship with God is a very personal thing, participation in the faith community is strictly optional.
- Baptism is the main event of the life of faith; everything after is just "icing on the cake."

Following the exercise, ask each person to identify the statement she/he felt most confused or uncertain about.

2. CONNECT 8 minutes

Distribute copies of the handout sheet along with pens or pencils. As you read the meanings of baptism out loud, ask participants to "rank" the meanings according to the importance they give to each one (1 = most important; 7 = least important).

Then ask:

- *Which is the most important meaning of baptism for you?*
- *Which is the least important meaning of baptism for you?*
- *Which meaning(s) of baptism had you never thought of before?*
- *Which meaning of baptism is still the most confusing or unclear to you now?*

Use information from the Insights from Scripture section to suggest appropriate answers.

3. EXPLORE THE BIBLE 8-10 minutes

Shift to this activity by saying: *If baptism seems kind of confusing, strange, or unnecessary, let's look at the baptism of someone who apparently thought it was pretty important.*

Explain that all Bible study begins with making simple observations about the passage. Ask everyone to turn to Mark 1:1-11 in their Bibles and ask for a volunteer to read as they follow along. Then ask:

- *In verse 1, Mark wants to be very clear that Jesus Christ is what?* (the Son of God)
- *In verses 2 and 3, whose coming fulfills the ancient prophecy of Isaiah?* (John the baptizer)
- *In verse 4, John proclaims a baptism of repentance for what?* (the forgiveness of sins)
- *In verse 5, all the people did what as they were baptized by John in the river Jordan?* (confessed their sins)
- *In verse 6, John was dressed like the prophet Elijah and must have been what to eat those locusts?* (very hungry, a little nutty, etc.)
- *In verse 7, John dramatizes the greater power of Jesus by saying he himself wasn't even worthy to perform the slave's job of what?* (removing the sandals from his master's feet)
- *In verse 8, John again acknowledges Jesus' greater power by saying his own baptism was "watered down" when compared to that of Jesus who will baptize with what?* (the Holy Spirit)
- *In verse 9, Jesus' baptism by John is startling because as we saw in verse 4, John's baptism was for what?* (the forgiveness of sins)
- *In verse 10, only Jesus sees what descending on him like a dove?* (the Spirit)
- *In verse 11, we readers are permitted to "overhear" God's establishment of Jesus' identity as what?* (Beloved Son)
- *What might Jesus' baptism have to do with ours?*

4. APPLY 10 minutes

Remind the group that John proclaimed "a baptism of repentance for the forgiveness of sins" (1:4) and Jesus said "Repent, and believe in the good news" (1:15). In other words, to be a disciple means repenting and committing. Ask participants what they think "repentance" means. Write key words on a chalkboard or newsprint. Now say:

- *Repentance is not just feeling sorry for wrongdoing; it is the conscious act of **turning away** from one's rebellion against God and **returning** to a right relationship with God.*
- *This right relationship with God is what the Bible means by "salvation." Salvation is a living relationship with God, not a frozen moment in time.*
- *Baptism expresses our readiness to repent, publicly confess our faults, receive forgiveness, and return to a right relationship with God (i.e. experience salvation) through Jesus Christ.*
- *Baptism dramatizes our **dying** to the old life (i.e., going under the water) and **rising** to the new life of membership and ministry within the body of Christ (i.e., coming up out of the water).*
- *Because baptism is the **beginning** of our faith identity and discipleship, it requires genuine repentance and commitment, not moral perfection.*

Pass out washable markers and ask everyone to write WITH GOD'S HELP, I WILL TURN AWAY FROM... somewhere **on their hand**. Invite them to complete the statement by writing down the thoughts, attitudes, and/or behaviors they need to "turn away" from every day to more fully return to a right relationship with God. Suggest that when they are finished writing, they may wish to quietly pray for God's grace and strength to repent of the things they have written.

5. **RESPOND** 10 minutes

Now turn to the baptismal questions on the right-hand side of the handout sheet. Explain that these vows are examples and not used in every baptismal service. As they ponder the questions, place the basin with water, towel, and soap either in the center of your circle or at the front of the room. (Add a mini-lecture about adult and child baptisms in the Catholic Church, if it seems good to do so, using information at the end of Insights.)

After several moments, invite sharing of questions, feelings, or concerns. Suggest that they keep this sheet in their Bibles at the beginning of Mark's Gospel to remind them of this study, the meaning of baptism, and the baptismal vows they have already made or may someday choose to make.

Then invite people to come one at a time to wash their hands, scrubbing off what they wrote earlier. Ask other group members to pray silently for each person as they come forward to wash up. When everyone, including you, has washed, hold hands in a circle, and say something like:

- *For those of you who've already been baptized into the body of Christ, I encourage you to reflect on the meaning of that decision now in light of what you've learned during our study of Mark's Gospel. We learned that being a disciple **doesn't** mean moral perfection, but it means being willing to get in the boat. It means listening for when you are called. It means getting rid of distractions and traveling light on the journey. Being a disciple means repenting. It means making a public commitment.*

- *For those of you who have not made the decision to be baptized into the body of Christ, I encourage you to seriously consider making such a commitment, recognizing that baptism is the beginning, not the completion, of your faith journey.*

Conclude with the following prayer:

Like your disciples of old, Lord Jesus,
  we continue to stumble along in our following of you.
Yet you continue to call us:
  to get in the boat and set out to sea;
  to drop our nets and follow where you lead;
  to deny ourselves and experience the good life God intends for us;
  to travel light as we continue your work in the world;
  to turn away from our sin and return to you;
  to join the faith community and begin the adventure of faithful discipleship.

Be near us, Lord Jesus,
  that on the calmest of seas and in the darkest of storms,
  we may see you more clearly, follow you more nearly,
  and love you more dearly, day by day.
And all God's people said, "AMEN."

 # INSIGHTS FROM SCRIPTURE

Though it has no shepherds keeping watch over their flocks by night, Mark 1:1-8 is clearly an Advent text because it announces the coming of Jesus Christ into a world that will clearly never be the same. Jesus' baptism was the inauguration of the ministry that would change the world.

» BAPTISM FOR REPENTANCE

As popularly understood, repentance is feeling sorry for some wrong committed. But those who came to John the Baptist had to be more than sorry. In New Testament Greek, to repent literally means "to change one's mind." This, together with the Hebrew verb meaning "to turn around," indicates that repentance involves a radical change of heart, will, and behavior. It is a fundamental turning of one's life away from sin and back to God. When John baptized for the repentance of sins, he did not mean for people to simply get a new feeling of clean, like on a soap commercial, but for them to make major changes in their attitudes and life orientations.

Water baptism was not new to the Jews. When Gentiles converted to Judaism, they had to undergo baptism as a symbolic cleansing for their past life. Ritual washing and purification was faithfully observed in all segments of Jewish life. What was new was the introduction of the Holy Spirit to baptism.

» LIKE A DOVE

Although the dove is nowhere directly associated with the Holy Spirit, there are rabbinical texts that compare the Holy Spirit to a dove or other bird. The phrase "like a dove" is more likely a reference to the Spirit's hovering motion than to its bodily form (by contrast, see Luke 3:22). The appearance of the dove at Jesus' baptism signified that the Spirit-famine was ended, the prophesies were fulfilled, and the Spirit was alive and at work in the ministry of Jesus. Eventually, baptism became the sign of membership in the Christian community as circumcision was the sign of membership in the Jewish community.

» WHAT ABOUT TODAY?

Society has become so individualized and compartmentalized that it is difficult to find a place to belong. Many youth have little understanding or appreciation of the parish's role or value in their lives. Understanding baptism as the sign of membership in a covenant community to which they belong and are accountable may appeal to their need for meaningful connections in a disconnected world.

Youth today are searching for identity but may be discouraged from finding it in a church that doesn't always "practice what it preaches." Understanding baptism as the *beginning* of Christian identity and discipleship that requires genuine repentance and commitment, not moral perfection, may provide a bridge between the realities and dreams of Christian discipleship.

As children of God, we follow wherever Jesus goes, knowing he will eventually take us to the very heart of God.

For more on how Catholics understand baptism, see the *Catechism of the Catholic Church:*

CCC: #386-421, 1212-1284

» THE BOTTOM LINE

Baptism establishes *Jesus'* identity as the Beloved Son of God and *our* identity as "children of God...Abraham's offspring, and heirs according to promise" (Gal. 3:26-29). With this assurance, we may follow wherever Jesus goes, knowing he will eventually take us to the very heart of God.

» ACTIVITY SUPPLEMENT

If you feel your group could benefit from learning about adult and infant baptism in the Catholic Church, include this mini-lecture along with the other Respond activities.

- The sacrament of baptism has evolved over the last 2,000 years. A good way to think of it now is as a **doorway into the Catholic Church** and as a **public marker** of someone's commitment to follow Jesus.
- **Is baptism for adults or infants**? The answer is "both," and "it depends."
    - In the Bible and in the first 200 years of Christianity, baptism was almost exclusively for adults. However, when the emperor Constantine converted to Christianity in 313 A.D., being Christian became fashionable instead of radical and dangerous.
    - Around the same time, St. Augustine developed the concept of **original sin**, which made infant baptism common.
    - Now that we emphasize the sacrament as a doorway into a community of faith, **Catholics welcome infants, children, or adults of any age to baptism**.
- So baptism:
    - **washes away our sin**,
    - makes us **adopted children of God**, and
    - makes us **members of the Body of Christ**.

More Than Getting Wet, Baptism Is...

In Real Life
Exploring tough questions facing youth today

- **A response to God's saving act through the life, death, and resurrection of Jesus Christ**
  It means turning toward God, being forgiven, and receiving the strength of the Holy Spirit (Acts 2:37-39).

- **An act of obedience to the teachings and example of Jesus Christ**
  Jesus was baptized, and the New Testament calls all who believe to be baptized (Mark 16:16).

- **A symbol of cleansing and new life**
  It is an outward sign of an inner experience. There is a new creation, a new birth (2 Cor. 5:17).

- **A public witness of the covenant relationship with God**
  Baptism is the sign of membership in the discipleship community (Eph. 4:4-6).

- **A commitment to become part of a witnessing Christian community, the body of Christ**
  Baptism is the moment of entering the church, of assuming responsible membership (1 Cor. 12:13).

- **A witness to the transforming power of the Holy Spirit in the believer's life**
  As they join the church through baptism, every Christian demonstrates an openness to the power of the Spirit (Rom. 12:2, Gal. 3:26-29, Eph. 4:5).

- **A beginning**
  It is understood not as something completed but as the start of a pilgrimage of faith (Rom. 6:4).

Promises of Baptism

- Do you renounce Satan and all his works and all his empty promises?

- Do you believe in God, the Father almighty, Creator of heaven and earth?

- Do you belileve in Jesus Christ, His only Son, our Lord, who was born into this world and suffered for us?

- Do you believe in the Holy Spirit, the holy catholic Church, the communion of saints, the forgiveness of sins, the resurrection of the body, and life everlasting?

OR

- Do you believe in Jesus Christ as the example of God's compassion who demonstrates the power of human connection and life as intended by God?

- Will you take your life pattern from Jesus, and will you learn his Way, repent of wrong, receive God's forgiveness, and live in the light?

- Will you be loyal to the church, upholding it by your prayers and your presence, your substance and your service?

>>>
Being a disciple doesn't mean moral perfection, but it means being willing to get in the boat. It means listening for when you are called. It means getting rid of distractions and traveling light on the journey. Being a disciple means repenting. It means making a public commitment.

Clueless and Called : Session 5

Permission is granted to photocopy this handout for use with this session.

⟩⟩⟩ EXTENDER SESSION
(Best used after Session 4)

ENTERTAINING ANGELS

⟩⟩ SESSION GOAL
Challenge participants to a more radical Christian discipleship through stories and images of ordinary people following Jesus in extraordinary ways.

⟩⟩ PLAN
If possible, arrange to meet for at least two and a half hours, view the video, and lead a discussion. A detailed study guide can be found at https://www.catholicvideo.com/files/EntertainAngels.pdf

If you have a more limited time for discussion, you may wish to use the following questions.

QUESTIONS FOR DISCUSSION

- What is the one word that best describes your reaction to this video?
- What in the video were you most inspired by?
- What in the video were you most bothered by?
- Dorothy Day confronted Jesus on the cross by telling him how hard he is to love in the drunks, the people who have lice and tuberculosis, those who wet their pants and who are smelly. What is your reaction to her challenge and even accusations of Jesus in that scene?
- In your experience who have been the hardest people to love in your life? Why? Who else do you imagine would be hard to love if you encountered them? Why?
- Jesus surrounded himself with a community of twelve ordinary people. Dorothy Day surrounded herself with others who wanted to follow Jesus by living in community with the poor. She realized she couldn't do it on her own. How can being a part of a faith community help you to follow Jesus more closely?

⟩⟩ Materials needed and advance preparation

- Order *Entertaining Angels: The Dorothy Day Story* DVD or arrange to stream it well before the date of the Extender Session. It is 1 hour and 52 minutes long.

- Equipment for showing the video. Arrange for the group to meet in an informal, comfortable setting for the session, perhaps in a home.

In Real Life
Exploring tough questions facing youth today

CLUELESS AND CALLED
Discipleship and the Gospel of Mark

What does it take to be a disciple? This study of the Gospel of Mark focuses on the requirements for following Jesus' way and the abundant life that is ours as a result. (5 sessions)

DO MIRACLES HAPPEN?
Signs and Wonders in the Gospel of John

The greatest miracle, recorded in John 1:14 and 3:16, is the miracle of God's love that became flesh and lived among us. But John also included examples of what we more traditionally think of as miracles: the wonder of abundance from little; healing; signs of impossibility and faith; and the resurrection. (5 sessions)

DO THE RIGHT THING
Ethics Shaped by Faith

How do you know what's right and what's wrong? Even when you figure it out, the right thing is often the unpopular or unpleasant choice. This unit offers participants a clearer sense of what it means to claim a faith identity, a foundation that can help them sort out the gritty details of ethics shaped by faith. (6 sessions)

FIGHT RIGHT
A Christian Approach to Conflict Resolution

This unit will help youth understand conflict and its function. They will learn how they can be honest and loving, and explore how conflict can be used for positive results. They will also learn ways to enhance their communication skills. 1 Corinthians. (5 sessions)

GOD IS A WARRIOR?
Violence in the Bible

The Bible challenges us to be reconciled to one another and work for justice. So what do we do with the stories that seem to condone violence or even encourage it? A discussion of issues in the Old and New Testaments. (6 sessions)

HOW DO YOU KNOW?
Wisdom in the Bible

Wisdom literature teaches us that we gain knowledge of the world, ourselves, and God through experience and observation. This unit provides practical, hands-on wisdom to help young people avoid life's snares and grow closer to God. Proverbs, Job, Ecclesiastes. (5 sessions)

HOW TO BE A TRUE FRIEND
The Bible Reveals Friendship's Heart

To be a friend takes skill. Help youth discover the secrets of friendship through various stories from the Old and New Testament. (6 sessions)

HOW TO READ THE BIBLE
Building Skills for Bible Study

What kind of book is the Bible? What does this book mean to me? This unit looks at the Bible as revelation, as history, as literature. Selected scripture. (5 sessions)

KEEPING THE GARDEN
A Faith Response to God's Creation

If Christians believe that God made the world, we do not need any more compelling reason to care for it than that God has handed us a treasure to hold and protect. This unit gets beyond trendy environmentalism and challenges youth to see environmental awareness as a religious issue. Genesis. (6 sessions)

MANTRAS, MENORAHS, AND MINARETS
Encountering Other Faiths

How is Christianity different from other faiths? Why do others believe the way they do? This study can give youth a new appreciation for the uniqueness of Jesus. Selected scripture. (5 sessions)

SALT, LIGHT, AND THE GOOD LIFE
The Beatitudes and the Sermon on the Mount

What can youth expect in a life of discipleship? This unit explores the Sermon on the Mount under four main sections: the Beatitudes, Salt and Light, Jesus and the Law, and Heavenly Teachings. Matthew 5. (6 sessions)

A SPECK IN THE UNIVERSE
The Bible on Self-Esteem and Peer Pressure

Discover God's unconditional love and acceptance of all people. This study will show positive ways to have one's life make a difference, and help youth find ways to resist negative peer pressure and turn it into positive action. (6 sessions)

THE RADICAL REIGN
Parables of Jesus

Jesus used parables to reveal what the kingdom of God is like, and how God relates to us. This study highlights how the parables reveal God's reign as radically different from the world we live in, and what that means for the Christian life. (6 sessions)

TESTING THE WATERS
Basic Tenets of Faith

Discover the biblical roots for the central Christian concepts of covenant, community, and baptism. This short course is a way to test the (baptismal) waters of Christianity before diving in, or review the basics for those who already have. (6 sessions)

WHO IS GOD?
Engaging the Mystery

God is beyond human comprehension, yet desires to be known. These sessions focus on the way we get clues about and glimpses of God from the Bible, God's creation, and church tradition. Selected scripture. (5 sessions)

www.ingramcontent.com/pod-product-compliance
Lightning Source LLC
Chambersburg PA
CBHW080408170426
43193CB00016B/2852